THE BLUE

for Christine,
thanks for your support
+ good to "share time"
with you
love
Kev Fegan
x

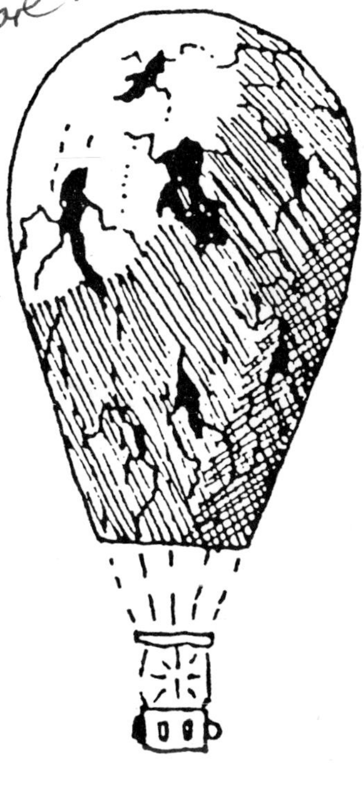

POEMS BY KEV FEGAN

Illustrations including cover by Peter Lane, c/o Stocken Prison.

"Public Enemy No.1" first published in **"The New Statesman"**.
"One Arm Bandit" broadcast on **"Word of Mouth"** (Border TV)

First published in 1988 by;
THE AMAZING COLOSSAL PRESS,
C/O 18 Hind Street, Retford, Notts. DN22 7EN
Telephone (0777) 700248.

Second Edition Printed March 1990.
With financial assistance from **EAST MIDLANDS ARTS.**

Typeset, Printed and Bound by:
THE BOOK PRESS
Nottingham.
(0602) 459405

Special thanks to:
Chris Frost, Education Officer, and the education staff at Stocken;
Lynne Hapgood and Debbie Hicks, East Midlands Arts;
Anne Peaker; East Midlands SHAPE; Henry Normal, Paul Cookson, Darren Poyzer.
... and especially: Peter Lane, Paul, Warren, Don, Tone, Tom, Jim, Simon, Phil, Sadique, Alex and all the men detained at Stocken Prison.

H.M. Prison Stocken in Leicestershire is a "Category C" prison containing some 300 adult male prisoners serving sentences between 18 months and life.

DEDICATION

This book is dedicated to prisoner 789959, Anthony Alexandrowicz, in his 19th year of a Life Sentence for aggravated burglary and G.B.H. There is, to my mind, more than reasonable doubt about whether "Alex" is actually guilty of the crime for which he has been convicted. The extraordinary length of his imprisonment in relation to the crime demands, at the very least, a Home Office enquiry and an Independent Judicial Review.

K.F.

INTRODUCTION

Working as a writer in a prison is perverse, which doesn't mean to say it isn't both rewarding and useful. It is like emigrating to another country with its own customs, routines, authorities, clothes and language. I have been immersed in both prison law and prison lore and I have struggled against the overwhelming paranoia of this strange culture.

During the year I have enjoyed the company of the men and their writing. Creative writing in prison takes on a very real meaning. On the 'great outside' we can play with words and explore the aesthetics of language; but for many prisoners it is a way of understanding themselves and coming to terms with their predicament.

I am pleased to have retained my integrity as a civilian and won the trust of the men with whom I have come into contact. It is a privileged position as a writer in prison because prisoners are able to talk to me informally.

The British penal system is lazy and unimaginative in its approach to sentencing; but, most of all, it does not sufficiently recognise the changes which occur in, particularly, long-term prisoners.

The rehabilitation which happens in spite of the penal system (and not because of it) is endangered the longer the man is kept in prison. If nothing else this work has taught me that long-term sentences are too long.

CONTENTS

Page

THE EMIGRANT

Dear ma,

I'm not very good at the writing
and I don't want to sound affected
but I'm having trouble fitting in here,
it's nothing like what I expected.

I would dearly love to send you
home a good few pence
but the money is so poor
with all the men paying no rent.

The mashed potatoes are lumpy,
the meat is like shoe - leather
and the tea is crude diesel -
it's a poor diet for a young fella.

The portions are barely enough
to sustain us to do our tasks
and, sure, we're given no idea
how long all this is to last.

Alcohol is banned here
but many of the boys brew
their own hooch and there is a steady
supply of other natural roots;

although black market prices
prohibit regular excesses.
The basis of all trade is tobacco
since money is so scarce.

An elaborate economy
has developed where most things can be
obtained. If you've the means to pay
there are all manner of luxuries.

All of our clothes are dyed blue
while the bossmen dress in black -
I find both colours depressing.
I long for the green corduroy jacket

I had back in the old country.
It is seen as a great offence
if you don't acknowledge everyone
every time you meet. The reticence

I have seen men fight over
or what they thought was behind
a blank look while the bossmen acknowledge
us only when they've a mind to.

Everyone is agreed that nothing
happens here without a reason:
it's not God but paranoia
that's elevated to a religion.

There is a permanent curfew
in the evening and the men
are kept in separate camps
to the women. I imagine

they don't want the cons (as we're called)
to propagate in great numbers,
they have no homogenous sense
of keeping a family together.

I am slowly learning the language:
there are a thousand words for dissent.
The vocabulary is very strange:
I got into trouble recently

for thinking jam - roll was the dessert.
There is a strong oral tradition here:
apparently, this system has been
around for thousands of years.

There are countless tales of men
escaping from this insecure place
into the land where the bossmen live;
but seldom is there a case

of a man returning home the same person.
Living in camps, what little we see
of the surrounding landscape leads
me to think that this country

is not exactly what I'd call beautiful.
The emigrants tend to group according
to the nature of their business
rather than their country of origin.

They say the longer a man stays here
the less likely he is to return and
I say, I would have to die first before
I put down roots in this foreign land.

I'll say goodbye now ma, I hope
this letter slips past the censor.
There's no way of knowing if you'll
receive it, with love,

your dearest son.

THE TAKING OF LIFE

Travelling back on my motor - bike from prison
I collided with a bird.
A beautiful corpse perched
on the air filter.
I did not want to kill it
we crossed visions.
It could quite easily have worried
me off my mechanical perch
and I would have ended in the ditch.
I could not pass it off as loose tar
with its yellow and black wingbar
and blood - red - head.

I wondered if this was its natural colour.
I looked it up when I arrived home
(to see if it was something
important in the bird world).
GOLDFINCH: a popular cage - bird
protected by law
frequents waste - grounds
its nest is woven of lichen and leaves
and it deliberately decorates that which it thieves.
A paranoid bird: only its song betrays
its presence, foregoing notes like wind - bells
but badly named as gold

is only seen clearly
on its wings in flight.
I took off my red helmet
which was splattered with flies.
A cloth and my conscience was wiped
clean. There are too many
to contemplate and no apparent
way to avoid collision
so their suffering becomes a nuisance
their number forgotten
but the Goldfinch
I will lament.

GREASY POLE

"Tone,
what are you doing in here?"
" Making apple turnovers -
what does it look like ?
What are you doing here ?"
" I've come to help you express yourself,"
" Fuck that !"

What I can't understand is why
I'm out and you're in ?
I suppose it went something like this :
at the Summer Fayre
they had a 30 foot greasy pole.
You used to launch yourself up this pole
only to slither down every time.
Everyone knew the pole was a trick;
but no - one else dare.
And you'd do anything for a dare:
" I dare you to eat that
apple - cog covered in dog shit."
" I dare you to run across
both carriages of that motorway."
" I dare you to batter that old queer."

And I've come to teach you
what you already know.
And I've come to teach you
what you already feel.
And I've come to teach you
what I can't teach myself.

POOR YORICK

A human skull
behind bars
is dead
and desperately needs a smoke

a human skull
behind bars
is paranoid
about people peering inside its head

a human skull
behind bars
eats worms
before they eat him

a human skull
behind bars
is a Shakespearian fool
and sips claret with Lord Byron

a human skull
behind bars
sees a butterfly emerge from
a cocoon like a warehouse burglar

a human skull
behind bars
understands silence
and is a testament to civilisation

ONE - ARM BANDIT

When things get out of hand
he grips the machine in an arm - lock
as he has done many times before
and pumps a little money into the slot.
The machine lights up: inside
he has 300 men on 'HOLD'.
He presses a few buttons
and the machine responds.
At least he has a choice:
a chance of winning.
A hundred cells are torn apart
when he decides to spin
and searched for selected treasure.
Nothing is found
but arrests are made
and he is down
the block again twisting
arms until someone admits
it won't pay out,
the machine is fixed,
it can't pay out.
Looking for a pattern
won't get him a result.
When all the money has gone
with a lengthy kick
he exits from the scene
before he is done for assault
and the lights go out on the fruit - machine

A LONG - TERM RELATIONSHIP

Over the years
I have grown very hard and dry
like red clay in the hot sun,
the water has evaporated
behind my blue eyes
and turned them grey.
When I first became locked
into this dark relationship
I was determined it would not
change me: we would live together
but I would retain
my separate identity.
I tried ignoring his attempts
to alter my little habit
of painting rainbows on the walls
and flared up when he saw fit
to contain me in artificial light;
but slowly with the discoloration
of time I was forced to compromise
and agreed to hand over my opaque
personality to him.
So much so that when
I open my mouth we talk
when I act we perform
and when I leave him
as eventually I must
I will be unable to speak
unable to act
I will be achromatized.

DEAR JOHN - an open letter by the Right Honorable Home Secretary to the 50,000 or so prisoners currently detained in Her Majesty's prisons throughout the British Isles.

Look, I've just lost patience
I don't want anything to do with you
any more
you can forget about the kids
and no access -
as far as they're concerned
you don't exist.
I don't want to know
what you're going through -
prison isn't meant to be a happy place,
you can write me all the letters you want
I won't read them.
You get a couple of quid a week,
free board and lodgings
I mean, what more could you want?
There's a lot of people out here
would welcome it
and don't think that this letter
gives you some sort of right
to smash up your cell,
if you want to do your bird
down the block
that's up to you
and if you're brutalised, well,
whose fault is it you're in there
in the first place?

And remember,
you do have the right to complain
in writing
and the right of appeal
in writing
and there's always the Board of Visitors.
If you behave yourself
you could get up to a third remission,
parole isn't quite what it appears
for those serving more than five years
but you can always live in hope,
can't you ?
Don't look to me for help
when you're eventually released
(if you're eventually released).
Listen, I'm not writing this
out of malice
or any desire for revenge,
it's for your own good.
You can't expect any help,
not now,
it's too late for rehabilitation.
Anyway, once a criminal
always a criminal,
that's what I say.

LADY AMPHETAMINE

when i lie on my back
and look up at the sky
i could be anywhere

i could quite easily
be lying beside you:
a romantic affair

alongside a river
where the sun warms me like
a bottle of red wine

your skin's a cool yellow
chamois leather and love
is an amphetamine:

snort it through a rolled-up
rizla 'til it explodes
with a spark in your eye

and make the most of it
because we both might be
in prison by Friday

you are fire, i'm paper:
when your first flames touch, they
burn from the outside in

there is cracking like bones
in an open fire as
your flames engulf my skin

a dream is cremated
and a desire is born -
of this i am aware

i'm lying on my back
looking up at the night
i could be anywhere

THE VISIT

I hear you are coming to visit me
so I tidy my room, several times,
arrange my desk into an altar
with pictures of you and
I wait for days .....

I can see you baptised in the river
with a bottle of wine in one hand
and a book in the other: you hang
from them as we kiss underwater
to hide our tears and stem their flow.

Your letters are pinned in the shape
of a crucifix on the notice board.
I have a piece of your lace
speared into the Judas hole in the door.
I hope you wear the chain I stole for you.

I was always a bad thief
and you were good at stealing hearts.
We will talk about climbing the hill where
the river begins and consider when
we might come out of hiding.

I suspect you love me for who
I am but I cannot know until
you visit me again. I wonder what
will become of us? Why
don't you come? Why don't you come?

ALL NICE PEOPLE

"They're all nice people," says Paul.

We come to talk to you
and refer to you as inmates not cons
we tell you you're articulate fellows
and ask for your opinions
we tour the prison
and leer into a single cell
like a 50 pence peep - show
(when holidaying in London
we always make a point of visiting Soho)
we introduce you to the arts
and the correct way of holding a tuning fork
we compliment you on how widely read you are
hang your paintings on our wall
and praise your poems
and when your case comes up for review
we are concerned about your welfare -
what will you do when you get out ?
where will you go ?
we understand your need for a release date
and promise to discuss it with the Panel -
next time -
we are impressed by any sign of remorse
we are proud of you.

PUBLIC ENEMY NO. 1

"Okay God, we know you're in there: you're surrounded so throw out your weapons and come out with your hands together in prayer. We're a reasonable people: it took you seven days to get yourself into this mess so you've got seven days to come out."

Day 1 -
we talk to you
in our best police voice:
no response.

Day 2 -
we talk some more
only this time kind of threatening:
no response

Day 3 -
we shoot out a few of your windows
try to loosen your tongue a little:
still no response

Day 4 -
we do nothing
play cards, worship a few idols maybe:
you send out a few prophets to negotiate.

Day 5 -
we get nowhere with the prophets
we need to speak to the boss:
you send out a book.

Day 6 -
only just learning to read
can't make sense of the book:
you send out your son.

Day 7 -
we shoot your son in self - defence
he appeared to be reaching into his pocket for a gun:
we await your response.

Day 8 -
we're expecting a shoot - out any minute now
either that or you've slipped out the back way
past the police and priests.

THE RECIDIVIST

I've been preparing my farewell speech
from the landing:
this place is full of gangsters -
you're all going somewhere like Papillon,
going to be somebody like Al Capone.
Now I'm not saying I'm a kleptomaniac
but I'd steal the smoke from your cigarette
I'm not saying I'm institutionalised
but I don't even bother trying doors any more
I'm not saying I'm cabbaging but prison's not so bad:
I like my big blue mug of tea
and crapping behind half a toilet door.
I know the score: of course there's freedom
of movement - if you get permission first.
I know what they're trying to do:
Dispersals to kick the shit out of me
then 'Cat.B' to fill me full of shit again
'Cat.C' to see if I can cope with petty rules
and 'Cat.D' to see if I can cope with even pettier rules.
But I can beat them at their own game, me:
you see, I'm a recidivist -
which really fucks up their system.
They don't know what to do with me.
No matter where they put me I re - offend.
Lock me in the Tower of London or the Savoy Hotel
after a few weeks of the open English climate
I'm back in again.
I'm not a danger to society
I'm an embarrassment.
I'm living proof their penal system doesn't work.

THE SMELL OF RELEASE

IT wants out
IT doesn't want to know
about what IT's going to do
when IT's released
IT, for some reason,
cannot concentrate
on studying for an O.U. credit
IT wants out
IT needs a holiday
long - term bird
does your head in
can't you understand ?
don't fill IT with
uncertainties
all IT needs
is a date
an E.D.R. *
all IT needs
is a little control
IT can't be doing with
parole and knock - backs
IT's all bollocks
IT wants out !

* (earliest date of release)

SMILE AS YOU GO UNDER

When you sail your small boat out to sea
in search of gold or a pleasure cruise,
when you're old enough to know you have nothing to lose
but you're secretly hoping to discover new territory
and half way across your crew mutinies,
sets you on a dingy and leaves you afloat
in a storm with a hole in your boat,
get up off your hands and knees
turn to the rising water
and smile as you go under.

    When you shoot your shuttle into outer space
    hoping to touch the furthest star
    or put the green back into Mars
    and the other members of the human race
    all die, leaving you alone with a monkey
    which you can only talk to
    via a v.d.u. and your space - suit
    has only enough oxygen until Monday,
    take a deep breath, space voyager,
    and smile as you go under.

When you leave your familly to live on your own
hoping to find you're self - contained,
unfurnished, warm and connected to the mains
but you find it hard to make the flat your home
when it's lonely at night in the silence of the storm
and sheets of lightening cover your bed,
when you've all this love to give but instead
you hurt yourself and wish you could be reborn,
wait for the peaceful rain to follow the thunder
and smile as you go under.

INMATE - IN - RESIDENCE

Below sea - level
silence is essential
like a military submarine
it is best that little
or nothing is known
of your whereabouts or purpose.

You have to determine
your own mission
and expect no support
from the outside.

By day you bend your penitent way
through shoals of uniformed fish
along chartered waterways
with an occasional glimpse
through the periscope
when someone visits you.

By night all the doors are sealed
and the steel hulk sways gently
adrift with dreams and memories
or rocks with nightmares and hope.

Above sea - level
the noisy sun
I take for granted
will rise again
providing
I do nothing to offend it.

STRAIGHT - JACKET - POTATO

I don't know who put me in here:
I'm what they call
a straight - jacket - potato
with bitter and t i t d r s . .
w s e o t .
o . .
My ancestors were up,
dug
shipped across on the old boat
and transplanted alongside canals,
railways
and motorways.
I into this orange soil
dug deep
and discovered I had green roots
(much greener than I had imagined)
which germinated in a terror campaign
to drive the English out of my brain:
incendiary devices explod - in my h a
- ed e d,
I live in fear of unclaimed suitcases
and holdalls by my bed.
Now I'm interned here without habeas corpus:
they keep asking me questions
about being a potato.
They thought they'd got rid of us
after the famine.
I told them:
a poor crop doesn't mean we've disappeared
but
gone
underground . . . . .

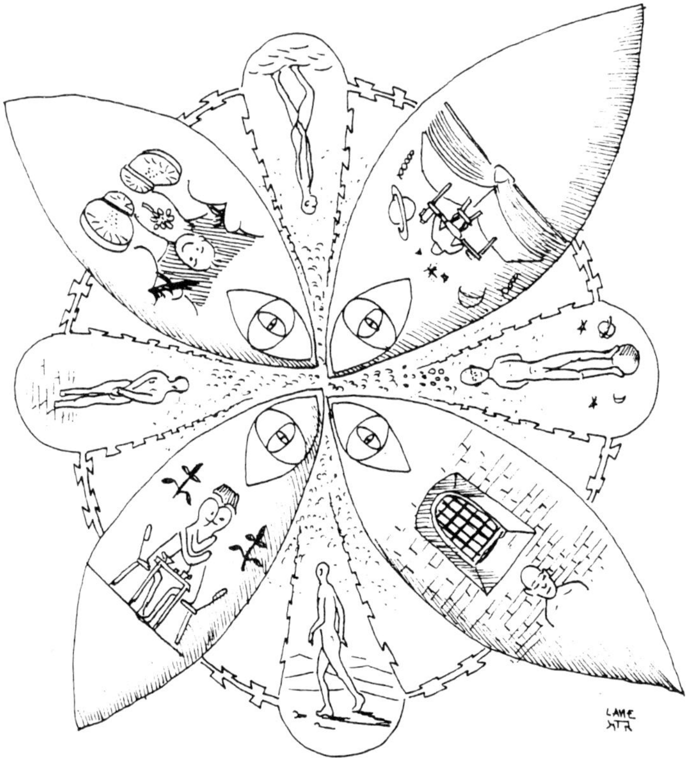
LANE

TIME - TRAVELLERS

supersonic aircraft crack like thunder across
the sky while behind the wire dreams
travel at twice the speed of sound
when you wake up in the morning
in your capsule that day is over
it no longer counts a digital display
of numbers repeat in your head
in your attempt to understand them
time is a journey across light years
and you are doing hard time
like discarded steel debris
spiralling through deep space
you divide your day and your capsule
into finite parts you stand on the ceiling
to perform your ablutions or climb along
corridors cleaning and crawling or hang
from the floor to study
open university and smoke
you plan a visit to earth
confirm a visit anticipate
the expressions on people's faces
and what you will talk about
eventually you let it happen
savour it for days weeks afterwards
stretch the event
until it sheds its significance
like a fuel tank from a shuttle
and you are doing hard time
like discarded steel debris
spiralling through deep space .....

PORTMERION SANDS

You could not be sure why we had brought you
to this strange village. Equipped with bucket
and spade it could have been a holiday
or a punishment. The blank villagers
appeared friendly. Past the Prisoner's house
under the eye of the Green Dome counting
the numbers of people making their way
to the estuary; but there was no sand.
So you took up your bucket to empty
the sea like a Sisyphean character
from tv mythology on the strength
of my promise that eventually you
would uncover a beach. And you laboured
in your absurdity while I waited,
omnisciently, for the tide to turn.
You had your beach and you built your castles
to defend your land against the blank sea
only to learn we are caught between tides.

FOLIE -A -DEUX

It was something they did
together like making a child

it wasn't as if one
of them was considered to blame

they led each other on
and each deviation became

more extreme than the last
until there was no turning back

his work involved selling
his audience increased
time for his family
was plotted on spread - sheets.

She waited for him to come home
like a father, husband

at times she made him wait for her
like a taxi, a man

she made do with second - hand goods
he needed to sell more

she tried much harder to give less
he wanted to give more

their crime wasn't neglect
but love died in their care
it was the final act
they performed together.

LONG - TERMERS' FAREWELL PARTY

mineral water in a bottle
and exotic fruits
cream cakes
and real cigarettes
cheese cut with a spoon
and celery nut salad
hob - nobs and farewell handshakes
yoghurt and optimism ....

THE LAST DAY

waiting in my one suit of clothes
for the electronic doors to open
the hardest part is leaving
others behind
i carry my few possessions
and clutch my Home Office Pass
equipped to face the world
i have my examples of writing
an experience i cannot transcribe
and a perverse nostalgia
for a perverse institution
i am leaving a better man
i am leaving a broken man

THE BLUE BALLOON

I woke up early one Winter morning a few years ago,
looked up at the sky and in place of the moon
there was something sinister overlooking my life
in the shape of a blue balloon.

I went to work a little later than usual
and was called into the office
where the boss warned me about timekeeping
and reminded me of my contractual promise.

I noticed behind his desk above the clock
in a corner of the room
an addition to the decor -
a picture of the blue balloon.

Walking home from work that night the same picture
appeared right across the city
on churches, shops, car parks, schools and even people's faces:
everywhere I looked something was watching me.

I thought no more about it until
one quiet afternoon
someone switched the television on
and there was the blue balloon.

A voice informed me that my back garden
was to be used as a nuclear base
for cruise missiles and satellite relay systems
to destroy the world from outer space.

It wasn't so much the sequestration of my land
as the fighting planned for my front room.
It occured to me I had little control over my life
and that it had something to do with the blue balloon.

The voice also spoke of several famines in the world,
of poverty, torture, and apartheid;
yet the record grain I produced at work was stored
in huge warehouses in crates marked 'human rights'.

I wanted to give away my surplus grain
and by - pass the blue balloon
but the voice said I didn't know how lucky I was
in not having to live under a red or black balloon.

There were people in my life
whom I cared for and I kissed
who would listen to my words
and label me 'anarchist'.

I decided that for some unknown reason
my friends must be immune
because they remarked that in all their obedient lives
they had never seen this blue balloon.

So I organised demonstrations
protesting at the suffering and waste
which was when the blue police first appeared
and beat us with truncheons and a High Court case.

I was taken in for questioning
and charged as a prophet of doom
I defended myself but when I opened my mouth
all that came out were blue balloons .....

Some time later I was given a better job and a faster car
no reason to complain,
I don't watch television any more
and I'd rather not think about grain.

Everyone needs to know their place
from the president to the bal - lunatic,
it might only exist inside your head
but everyone needs the blue balloon.

Everything was fine until that last party
when we were talking eye to eye
and stumbled across a rediscovery
about something that orders our lives.

Our conversation held hands
and tried to leave the room
but standing guard by the door
was the threat of the blue balloon.

There will come a day when the myth will burst
and we will learn to live without the blue balloon
and when I wake up to a Winter sky
all I will see is the moon.

" If this play doesn't become a standard text and Milner and Hay aren't recognised as two immensely talented performers then justice is in short supply which is the starting point of 'Rule 43'... Devastating theatre that demands superlatives, I can't praise it enough."

THE STAGE & TELEVISION TODAY

The Cracked Actors' Company
c/o The Actors' Centre
Little John Street
Manchester M3 4PQ
Bookings: 061 330 5681

THE AMAZING COLOSSAL PRESS

18 HIND ST., RETFORD, NOTTS, DN22 7EN.

PERSONAL VENDETTA

The poems of John Bitumen
A5, glossy cover, illustrated.
Price £ 1.50 (incl. p & p)

" Well crafted tragi - comic poetry, slick and highly perceptive.... pushes stand up poetry into new areas of sardonic observance. "

Manchester Evening News.

THE PRIVATE CRIMES OF NICK TOCZEK
(prose pieces)

A5, glossy cover, illustrated
Price £ 1.50 (incl. p & p)

All cheques / P.O.'s payable to " The Amazing Colossal Press "

PUBLISHED ON SEPTEMBER 1st 1990

NOW THEN DAVOS

A collection of performance poems, with commentary, by:

Ian McMillan
" Halfway to fame " (Independent on Sunday)

Martyn Wiley
" A natural comic " (Stockport Times)

David Harmer
" Our headmaster " (Rosedale Middle School News)

Both individually and as Circus of Poets, Ian McMillan, Martyn Wiley and David Harmer have performed their poetry in hundreds of venues since 1982. They have appeared in schools, theatres, pubs, arts centres, museums, fields, prisons and front rooms all over Britain.

Since 1982 audiences have been asking for a book of the performance poems, and since 1982 Ian, Martyn and David have been promising to do one. Now The Amazing Colossal Press have done it for them. Buy it and have your own Circus of Poets performance in the privacy of your own home.

Price £2.95 (incl. p & p)

All cheques / P.O.'s payable to " The Amazing Colossal Press "

THE
BLUE
BALLOON

KEVIN FEGAN, Poet and Playwright, is currently Arts Council Resident Dramatist with Welfare State International, working in Barrow - in - Furness on ' Shipyard Tales ' for July 1990. Kevin is well - known for his lively poetry readings to a wide variety of audiences. His work has been featured on television, radio and theatre and in various magazines, including ' The New Statesman ', and more recently in the international poetry series for television, ' Word of Mouth '. Recent plays include ' Private Times ' (The Library Theatre, Manchester), ' Rule 43 ' (The Cracked Actors' Company, national tour including British prisons), ' Upon St.George's Hill ' (The Monday Play, B.B.C.Radio 4), 'A' (Leicester Haymarket Theatre Studio) and ' McAlpine's Fusilier ' (Contact Theatre, Manchester). Plays coming up soon: ' Lord Dynamite ' (co - written with John Fox) and ' Matey Boy ' for Welfare State International, a third tour of ' Rule 43 ' in the autumn by Cracked Actors' Company and a play for schools published by John Murray, ' How Can I Put It ?'

Kevin is available for poetry readings and creative writing workshops.

Contact: 128 Brand Lane, Stanton Hill, Ashfield, Notts. NG17 3GH. Tel. (0623) 515235.